# POWDER TOWER

# POWDER TOWER

Jackie Wills

Arc
PUBLICATIONS
1995

Published by Arc Publications
Nanholme Mill, Shaw Wood Road
Todmorden, Lancs. OL14 6DA



Design by Tony Ward
Printed at Arc & Throstle Press
Nanholme Mill, Todmorden, Lancs

ISBN 0946407 86 X

Thanks to: *Slow Dancer* magazine and press, *Virago, The Oscars Press, Bedford Festival Anthology, Wide Skirt, The North, Poetry London Newsletter, Verse, Spokes, Kent and Sussex Poetry Anthology 1993, Honest Ulsterman, The Sunday Times, Agenda* who have published poems in this collection, and South East Arts for the bursary which enabled me to finish it.

*Dedicated to my mother, Risenga,
Mrisi and Giya*

The Publishers acknowledge financial assistance from Yorkshire and Humberside Arts Board

# Contents

# JAPONICA

Our house shuddered with bass lines
as my brother burst into his teens
like a skinhead emerging from a chrysalis.
Downstairs, watching tv, we'd feel the room vibrate –
dialogue drowned out as his filled with sound,
thick as the smoke from my father's non-stop cigarettes.
No-one dared knock on his locked door
we just turned the volume up
until it became a duel and when each record stopped
we'd rush for the set, ashamed to be caught out.
It could go on for hours until he went for a bath,
every towel left wet as a flannel on the floor.
When he came out, his face had been picked
into a mess of blotches and blood.

But he was the only one of us who knew the Latin names
of plants at ten, who'd asked for a patch of his own
in the garden, where he planted lettuce alongside daffodils
and night scented stock. He buried japonica apples
all along the fence one day because the pink flowers
were my mother's favourites. He took the dog
on a five mile walk across the common
the day it was put down and he knew why my father
had spent so many months at home
but never let on – just punched more holes
in each cheap plywood door.

## BREATH

When she wakes up between midnight
and seven, and listens,
she feels the room's become
one of those rubber balloons in hospitals,
monitoring breath as it inflates and flattens.

With three of them in there,
trying to separate the other strands
of breath, son's and husband's,
is like easing a thread
from a plaited skein of cotton to mend a tear.

## THE ROPEMAKERS

After stooping through a tunnel washed smooth by floods
our guide switches off the lights and we stand
still as stalagmites trying to guess where he is
from the strength of his sweet, beery breath, telling us
as if he's engineered it himself, there'll never be a crack
of sun or moon in here – where each winter three rivers
once collided and tons of water were forced upwards,
pummelling a ceiling more intricate than any stately home's.
Above, near the entrance, the ropemakers
lived – twisting and plaiting – and after rain or thaws,
had no need of ears, just mouthed and lipread
above the roar, their faces yellow in the candle flames
paled by daylight only a few hours a week.

The old Anglia can't take it and my parents' plans for driving
through the night give out with the engine in a sheet of rain.
By fluke my father finds a garage, a removals van
filling up, so we're lifted, floppy with tiredness,
into the back to lie on blankets in the dark. No signposts,
no blinding headlights for my father to swear at
when they won't dip, no orange glare at each new town –
just that rattle of a toolbox and roll down door.
They could be taking us anywhere.
My mother promises tomorrow she'll pick us cherries.
My brothers whisper themselves to sleep, but I know
why the ropemakers avoided that hole in the back
of their cave, so opaque, immune to wax and matches –
it could draw you in by accident,
commanding silence while skin slowly covered your eyes.

## KITE

Last night you buzzed in your sleep
like a motor without a spark.
Another nightmare, glass rubbed
on silk. You isolate yourself with covers
as if I'm about to strip the bed,
leave you naked as copper.

Sometimes I think you're lightning
looking for earth and I'm flying a kite
winching it back in the rain, scared by clouds
and early experiments with electricity
when a silver coated line was dragged
towards a storm like bait.

# FEEDING
*for my mother*

Her whispers turn to frost
on the window – thickening the glass.
Words settle into stars, forming
icy constellations, a frozen geometry
of nonsense; each angle, sharp
as the stab of milk coming in.

All her children were born in winter.
One followed the other,
to claim a quartet of days
between Christmas and spring.

The moon moves across the frame
from the harbour
until she can't see it anymore,
while she waits, shivering,
for the head to fall back, white dribble
overflowing from his swollen lips.

## FOREIGNER

Tomorrow you'll sit in your room
and outside the only movement will be litter.
You'll wander corridors of closed doors
and go to the cinema where you'll watch
the screen burst or flicker – hearing but most of the time
not understanding. You'll wish you could meet people
in cafés, at traffic lights, the way you do at home.
But you have just minutes to make yourself understood
before heads turn away.

And if you find a lover there'll be a time
when you hand her a book and ask her to read aloud,
because you need to hear her speak your language;
translating as she mispronounces words she's never heard.
And if you like her, maybe you'll wonder
how long you'll have to witness
the sounds of your country broken up
like this – all those pauses in the wrong place.

## COUNTING

Susan wants to attach scythes to the wheels
of her father's car and cut everyone off at the knees,
like Boadicea. She could flatten a town centre
as quickly as a combine harvester. She's referee
when I fight with Donna over a ruler; snapped,
beating a cage of locusts so they would try to escape.
As we smash each other against lockers, Susan counts.

Every thud on metal is a point. Outside the art room
she throttles me for losing and my throat stings with vomit
as an undigested pea is forced from my nostril.
When I jump on her head in the swimming pool
her gushing nose leaves a trail on the white tiles like steak
dripping inside our fridge. But we make peace in needlework,
sewing skirts short enough to be cut from remnants.

They will flap against our buttocks like shirt-tails
when we meet on Saturday in the Army and Navy café,
wrists smudged with lipstick – Fuchsia, Pink Passion,
Carnival, Hot Date. We put them on in the toilet mirror,
practising open-mouthed kisses on folded tissues –
the fine lines of our lips printed like the claws
of hungry birds treading lightly over snow.

# LOSING THE LIGHT

On the hottest day of August
he cat-walks the length of the beach
in a black linen suit,
not once getting it wet,
four gold chains burning
around his neck.

Their bodies slide over each other
in the heat like newly landed fish.
But as they kneel in front of her open fridge,
faces freckled yellow with lily pollen from the garden,
she sees smiling pumpkins big as bellies
with flames for eyes, her outside the tube
as the sky flares, the street cracks
and boys run laughing into the dark.
She'll never find him on Halloween.

## WAITING ROOM

While the fans fail to keep the thermometer
below 80 and the waiting room's emptier
than any time of the year, this woman's spent
half an hour between a problem page and eight
month old horoscope, plotting her past and matching
the month's prize letter to Astrid's January
predictions. Velvet December, satin New Year . . .
she's remembering the feel of his hands

smoothing fabrics over her hips during a two week
piss-up, then her on the phone every night
reciting the same letter, believing
she's brought it on herself as deliberately
as going to the shed for petrol
when the kids are upstairs and dribbling
it over her head until she's standing
in a puddle, stinking like a garage.

# WITNESS

Here, a clock keeps its own time –
the numbers have fallen from its face,
its arms buckle with the warped disc
as it slumps against a wall,
stopped at 5.20. It's all that marks
the entrance to a chamber of rafters,
pulleys, ropes and dark pits –
a foundry where bells hang silent
or stand cooling in moulds like dying tulip heads.

Spotlit, a woman bends over a workbench
piled high with tools, engraving,
her back to it all. She is one of those
who choose never to tell. I came here by mistake
and leave wondering where the numbers went –
whether they dropped one by one
the way you lose an hour now and then –
where they're buried,
whether a bell chimed on, regardless.

# OUT OF BOUNDS

Those pew chairs were rigid,
screwed together tight with batons –
you'd pull backwards, push forwards
but would never separate yourself
from that row of bowed heads.

If we could, we'd skive
to caves among the rhododendrons
and below their pink and purple balloons
read the Thoughts of Chairman Mao
or a dog-eared issue of Cosmo
with its famous full length male nude,
listening for the Geography master with his cane.

When it was safe,
we'd sneak into the nuns' graveyard,
ringed with roses and horse chestnuts,
reddening the grass around them.
It was out of bounds, taboo
as the lipstick we saw a Sister trying
in an upstairs window,
maybe because she wanted
some colour on her face, to be surprised
when she checked her veil in the mirror.

## SAILING TO GALLIPOLI

Looking over the landing craft
he sees the faces of his friends
pale as starfish
through a clear Marmara sea
and wonders if they will stay
staring at the sky
or be pulled by currents
through the Dardanelles, scattering
among islands in the Aegean.

Years later in a glass bottomed boat
cruising to a coral reef,
he remembers a bluebell wood
he saw from a motorway.
The flowers seemed to drain colour
from above the trees
and bring it back to earth –
so many he couldn't move
without stepping on them.

# STICKY FINGERS

Everyone in our street
knew about my best friend's mother
and the builder from around the corner.
I heard from behind the bannisters,
upstairs. It was the best place
to eavesdrop on parents' secrets.
I couldn't tell her. I thought if I said anything
it would be like stepping into that maze of netting
revealed in our garden on mornings
when the sun comes out early –
the criss-cross layer of webs
suspended from the tips of wet grass,
between leaves and stems of border plants,
joining branches of trees, and shining
as if it was drenched in mercury.
In a few hours, you could believe
it had been scorched away,
until your fingers stuck together slightly –
tiny threads wrapped around them.

# INTENSIVE CARE

The chaplain who arrived to give last rites
was drunk and C of E. The Catholic priest
carried a briefcase and was in a hurry
as if he knew mentioning miracles was risky.
Her father's body was tightening with poison –

colonies of toxins he couldn't repel.
The first time she touched him, nervous of disturbing
tubes taped on like grafts to a tree, he fought
towards consciousness with a grunt and shudder,
his mouth stuffed with a breathing pipe.

It was his last attempt – stronger tranquillisers
knocked him deeper into sleep. Drawing a curtain
would not muffle her voice, so she whispered,
but later remembered he was deaf in one ear.
Perhaps she imagined the twitch in the finger?

When his heart line stretched till there were no more
peaks, it was like a starter gun – threatening calls
pre-funeral, lies about money lent or given, claims
to his watch and wedding ring; her brothers
suddenly hooped around his home like a cordon.

# HAT TRICK

The fortune-teller sweats
as she speeds through her commentary
picking out prizes
the way I used to dip hands
into sawdust at village fetes
for a pistol or warped plastic mirror.
This time it's twins and confetti.
I went for the hat-trick,
cards, palm and crystal ball.
But later, comparing notes,
find my future's the same as Jane's.

So I drive to the pool
left behind by quarrymen
where trees have no reflections.
There could be carp below the leaves.
I imagine them moving slowly over mud.
Water fills vacuums faster than air
in this damp country.
No-one would dare fish here.

## DOWNSTREAM

It was the only thing that would stop
you crying. We'd stand under heavy-branched
trees to watch the dark green pool tugged
towards the weir, lightening as it flowed
over the concrete dam in a rush –
a litany of the villages it would pass
through, La Maurousse, Rochtrejoux.

The sun was so hot, you darkened in the shade.
On that cool bridge, I'd hold you tighter.
The pool looked so still, its dusty surface
suspended by weed, while stones rocked
slowly on the bottom. If I was careless,
we could be pulled over the weir, to float
downstream, to be found in the shallows.

# TYRE FACTORY

On the roof of the burnt out flats
someone's painted WAYNE in capitals
large as numbers on police patrols
which race round the estate after stolen Escorts.
Wayne's the five-a-side football star
a natural at technical drawing
but he's in a class of 35 – most mornings
hardly 20, and can strip a flat bare
before a coffin's in flames – he's in there quick
when old ladies die, seeing what's left to break
up or sell. The tyre factory, his dad's work,
is flattened, the ground still red with brick,
hammered into pebbles. Only the social club's
standing, its nicotined walls all there is to contain
old arguments about pay and profit – routines
redundant as the once weekly union subs.
And when bitter accusations of a sell-out
drown the barman shouting time
it's left to sons who've never worked to calm
fathers' friends as they stagger into the street –
further up, a teenage mother's taking cushions
off the sofa, looking among crumbs
and lost Lego for a few stray coins
to buy 10 Silk Cut; and a woman's
stuffing envelopes with offers of credit
at 27% interest until her eyes close.
But outside the shop in the precinct, built by a dubious
developer with the wrong mix of concrete,
the argument between Wayne and his friends
isn't about management victory and union loss
but which of the doors will be easier to force –
they've learned to net much better dividends.

# EATING ALONE

Raising his knees to dance
as he did when corn and mangoes grew
around his house, he remembers
his country's wedding songs
warning of the time, after cakes are eaten
and guests gone,
when divorces are made.

Frying onions and tomatoes
he throws in a fistful of the masonja
sent from home, curled as old hands,
some still sharp with spines. He brushes one
against his cheek.
Newly caught and stuffed in pockets
they'd scratch his legs raw
but dried, lasted all year,
through days without meat.

Spinning the whisk to thicken maize meal,
he celebrates the taste alone,
picking a gravy fattened one from the pan
and thinks of the long marimbas
it takes two to play – bass, treble and soprano –
how he'd beat notes out of wood
as if they were insects.

## HEAVY PETTING

The closest we got to sex education
apart from triangular sketches of tubes and womb,
charting the sperm's reptilian journey,
was when Father Walker instructed us
to think about French kissing.

He'd tell us with a wink, he only wore a cassock
when he was feeling unholy; and keep it on
for days. So you could tell him
about the party when Jimmy, smooth
as his trouser crease, took over the deck
around 10 pm to slip on Dock of the Bay,
dispersing us from our huddle
quicker than detergent on oil.

How, on the windowseat, he pressed
the bra-strap into your flesh, squeezing
finger and thumb as if it was a boil,
until it gave way and you noticed the cold
as he pushed you against the glass
his knee between yours.

You'd seen Father Walker comfort a girl,
pull her head towards him
the way a woman eases a baby onto her nipple.

## DOLLS

Before he began searching the common
for blanks from the firing range,
he cleared the loft for war games
and moulded plaster hills
large enough to hide battalions.
Each Saturday his army invaded more rafters

His first Christmas home – a mid tour break
his laugh was deeper
as he told us about mick baiting
in Republican pubs.
Minutes after we walked into the local
he'd spotted the other exit,
had his back to the wall
and we could have been those dolls
poking out of boxes,
squashed against the eaves –
a flamenco dancer, porcelain lady without arn
silent in their bunkers
while he claimed a table.

## TIDE

The tide's so far out, the sea's hovering
above land. You bend for a shell and smell perfume.
Sun burns waves to a hiss. You walk slowly, stopping
to see how far you've come, how far there is to go.

You expected more, but this sand swallows
everything. It's so shallow you'd have to wade
another 20 minutes to swim –
past the bar on the cliff, salty fields of sheep.

Your friends out of sight, suddenly this
isn't a beach. Waves are bigger, they're breaking
on your heels. Dips and channels fill up in front of you.
It seemed so flat. There's a river, waist deep.

A man leans out of a helicopter with a megaphone,
shouting, as you approach that band of mud
which sucks you down to your knees
and local people dig to fire into pots.

You could lie in it, be pulled into that dark seam
as the tide reclaims the land it lent you; rushes
to your friends with gifts of wood and plastic,
swirls around islands you didn't know about when you left.

## HIGH NOTES

*for Mrisi*

We lie him under the copper beech
on a mat and blankets
and watch the mime show
on the bowling green, neat
as fresh sheets; bodies which tip
and tilt, slowly uncurl, rock on the heels.

This is his first day out. We walk
slowly to the park, under the viaduct,
its arches like the reflections
in two mirrors, each curve repeating
itself until it bends out of sight,

past the copper gas lamps, fish
with enormous mouths, fat and fleshy,
the kind which grin in children's books
with curled tails and generous flippers;
past the statue where you pose, chest
out, his arms and legs dangling
from the sling sleepily.

We're beating the bounds
of his territory, the swings and bouncy
sheep which buck and rear
like unbroken horses.

A procession of women in bleached whites
smile at us. Their umbrellas,
fold away chairs, sparkling shandies
and rubber mats fill the greens.
We close our eyes, listening to the knock
of wood against wood, silencing the high notes.

## MARIGOLDS

He’s asleep. A bird’s flown
into silhouettes of branches
on the terrace wall.
It moves like a hand fluttering
in front of a candle
making monsters with its fingers.
I have gone from one man to another.

His clothes are drying
on a wooden horse.
I can see the green, red and grey
of the shirt he wore when we met.
In just half an hour the shadows have moved –
they’re closing the marigold petals,
stretching, drifting indoors.

# FAMILY

## i

I need to see earth again.
Corn and wheat turned over, dug in,
furrows even as textiles, reflecting nothing.
I'm exhausted by that half hovering way we live.
No time to sit under a tree
pick the skeleton from a leaf.

This morning a long cloud arched across the sky
breaking up at the edge, the way
fish scales separate when the body bends.
I passed the recreation ground
where I walked the dog in Levi button flies
and the phone box I used to ring boys.
Further on, the wood, hollow
with bricked up underground shafts.
And everywhere, elderberries hanging
upside down, dripping purple
as if mourning, into the mud.

The wood's haunted by black deer
which appear like shadows, then they're gone
as if they've been swallowed by a mine.
An arch, wide enough for a trolley, stands alone
among diseased maple trees.
Stripped of cables, winches, gears,
like a Roman monument, it's reverted to stone.

On the flood plain, in the valley
water and bank are patchy with down
but the swans have moved on,
down the river, under the bridge.

ii

I'm on the edge of a field
looking at houses on the hill.
It's old, veined like hands.
The sort of hill you see from a train
and never find again.

Today I saw my mother after 20 years.
There are lines in her face
as if water's been running over it.
Skin's patched on her arms, no longer
part of the flesh. It's coming off like paper.

She travelled, paced Paris
in shoes which crippled, drank champagne
on trains but never met
her father's African wife – just watched
cine-film on winter nights of wildlife shot
from landrovers and dusted
wooden antelope on her mantelpiece.

Singing in a band, I met a man
who could have been her brother –
his father was Scottish
but he'd kept his mother's name.
He could sing a roll call of generations.
He could talk to ancestors.

"Who are you?" he said. "How far back can you go?"

I can go no further than my grandfather
holding a drill in his hand
making old mouths shine
in a chalk coated attic
where he kept rows of teeth,
sized, and stuck to pink plastic.

iii

I don't know where I come from.
Relations are scattered all over the world.
It's a line rough with the knots of many diasporas.
An obscure cousin's research found a Huguenot connection,
a drunken Welsh doctor and Irish marriage certificate
signed with a cross.
My parents never passed on names.
So many came to this island or left to colonise.
Now the line's brittle as old glass –
which needs stroking to stay liquid.
Not even that silver watch remains,
only arguments about inheritance.

I was once on a moor, following streams
between six foot banks of black peat.
It could have been a maze
except this had no entrance or exit
you came in because you were lost.
I want to understand
this tradition of amnesia.
I want to find the ground
that hasn't been turned for centuries,
its legacy of anthrax, plague pit
and warning circles of trees.

## DOING THE RIGHT THING

Sometimes you have to stay in bed all day,
watch rain on the window, a yellow tree.
An office can be like a vice.
By the end of eight hours you've no breath left.
Sometimes going out is dangerous –
when you don't see cars.
A man can sleepwalk naked
down Mile End Road
hand over his genitals,
but no-one gives him a coat.
Just like those dreams you had as a child –
at school, in a nightdress,
with nothing underneath.

# BURNING THE STUBBLE

A farmer at the end of summer
brands squares into the dried gold
of his countryside
as if he's creating abstracts.
Driving to the sea,
I smell stalks burning,
those beds of nails left over
after combines have cut and threshed.
Smoke blows across the Downs.

These fields are ignited in lines
which advance the way a row of policemen
moves towards a crowd
with sunlight on their shields.
Even souls of the dead are caught here,
if it is true, as some believe,
they become butterflies.

## POWDER TOWER

Coming back is easy.
We can paddle the estuary
we waded chest high, clothes over our heads
to reach the dunes
see an occasional camel train.
Here freshwater turtles
die sparkling in salt,
herons fish with gulls.
Storms smashed the bridge
leaving only half a road.

It's getting dark.
Hassam and Mark climb
a ruined gunpowder tower
swapping languages – a pound
of oranges, the word for fig.
Listening to them struggle
I watch the horizon redden
as if I'm witnessing a battle
and the broken turret's arsenal
is exploding over the sea.

# IN HIDING

He laughs when she rakes over flowerbeds
searching for evidence of earlier
settlements – arrow heads, their edges
hammered millimetre by millimetre
neat as a circle of thumb marks in pastry.

Why bother, when stones jut viciously
out of paths – asking to be split open
the way a thrush bashes snail shells
to reach flesh. There has to be more inside,
an uneven circle of quartz or crystal.

As sun stretches trees across the lawn,
tops scraping the close boarded fence,
she watches him hold his chunk
of raw amethyst to the window
and he becomes Gulliver in Brobdingnag.

He shrinks among its spikes. It's as if
he's absorbed by the rock base, forced
upwards by osmosis, deepening the mauve
to a denser purple – the colour of the small
cut stone trapped in gold, he put around her neck.

# THE STREAM

When the water company opened
the sluice gates, it blocked off her escape –
obliterated footprints in the stream bed,
smashed her useless dams. Overnight, her route
into the woods away from the bordered, tidy garden,
disappeared. Instead, she had to watch her father
pull daisies from the closely mown lawn,
hammer a makeshift fence of branches
along the bank. Only he was allowed to jump
to the other side so he could trap
the vixen which screamed at night
like a woman and massacred the street's
fat rabbits and guinea pigs. She listened to him
shout 'slut' at her mother, smashing a glass
against the wall; caught them once in the kitchen
pulling apart from each other when they saw her,
as if they shouldn't be kissing.

# NIGHT FEAST

The smooth bannister's like skin
as I feel my way downstairs with my feet
the way a dancer learns a routine.

As the carpet levels out I turn right
and lift a hook from the kitchen door,
rubbing the wall then changing my mind.

This way there's only fridge light
to frame me crouching for cold potatoes,
mayonnaise, sagging trifle, curry.

I feel the cat's tail on my back
then her hard head, butting my hand
away from a bowl of herrings.

Upstairs the baby's asleep.
Weaned for six months, his mouth
still moves on a dreamed nipple.

## POPULAR SCENES OF LAKES

The tall iron cross recalls her emaciation.
Below it, what was a photo
set in marble, has become a whitewashed window
looking onto stone, a useless eye.
Only on the newest graves are portraits still clear.
They could be adverts for life. But month by month
the image promised when the shutter clicks
bleaches a little more – fleshy parts first,
then mouth, nose, until there's barely a feature left
in an outline which somehow persists.

This woman was willing to risk days
when she was so high up there'd be nothing but cloud,
for the comfort of knowing the name of every wheeling bird;
distaining the valley where mist clung
to the earth each morning like an unwanted friend.

Her country's being lost, to chalets
on keyrings, shops sticky with shiny, jellied cakes
and while she might not have mourned
the valley, with its tanneries selling miniature skins
like flying squirrels, she would have warned
her grandchildren, "Do not believe your own postcards."

# HAIR

The hairdresser's mirrors throw my body
back to me in bits. Feet, face, torso, move
independently under the colonnade holding up a café
where I sit on sunny days, counting
the unsuspecting heads of acquaintances,
as if they're a measure of belonging.

My first haircut after moving here,
there was half an inch difference ear to ear.
The bin bags outside are split by kicks; releasing
brown half moons, blown underfoot with leaves.
They should be wrapped up, like holiday snaps
sliding naked down a chute in the photoshop window.

Now my son sits on a chair and I cut quickly in a line
above my forefinger, careful not to let the fluffy curls
fall to the floor. His father puts them in an envelope,
as if we're preserving his emerging alphabet:
round vowels, curved consonants which cling
magnetically to the fridge, waiting for words.

# CARETAKER

On a rare day of rain she goes to the attic
and finds a dressmaker's litter of scraps –
under the eaves, bundles of half made clothes,
curtain cut into cushion squares,
a black lace and net party skirt,
velvet bolero, hem unstitched,
light woollen check edged in tailor's chalk.

It was as if she'd come home.
Once she'd buy lengths of fabric just on touch;
tightly woven cotton, soft as silk,
heavy, ridged Indian herringbone.
She could chart her adult life with it –
from her first nightdress with perfect seams,
to the dresses washed, worn and darned
until they cannot be retrieved.

But none shone like these circus costumes
in the candle as she pulls them from bags
releasing sweat, perfume and something sweet like dung.
She takes a scarf, heavy with brocade
in silver and gold. It will remind her
when she has saved enough to leave
she was a caretaker and one day, a thief.

# MIGRATION

When we're tired of blowing on ashes
to break them into flame
and our faces flatten in the dark,
we hear a spluttering –
like engines muffled by distance.
Geese are grazing the marsh
stripping tops from reeds
in the few hours they have
before daylight, when gunfire
will push them towards a mountain
which seems to crumble and rebuild itself
as thousands of us walk down, then up.

## CLIMBER

These roses marked my childhood boundary,
fell, armed, all over the fence
separating our house from next door.
Pink and full-headed, when you brushed past
or touched them, one would always burst.

I made rosewater with the petals.
They soaked in jam-jars for hours –
but bruised, darkening, threatening to rot
they bled something of their scent.
Later I read in a magazine
it was good for the skin.

I would fill a room with them
if I had a garden.
Flowers reach deep into the lungs
to the first days of consciousness,
a world seen upside down.
It's like a finger tracing my spine
someone blowing on my neck
as if he's giving me his breath.

## HOMING

### i

She rented a house with three bedrooms
but my brothers never visited her, or the flat
she later bought with the divorce money.
It was a cold house with thin walls and mean
strip of lawn out back, a car port at the front.
The man next door kept pigeons. She'd listen
to their throaty sounds, soft as down
drifting from the shed and think of children
making up codes. She tried to ring my brothers
but my father always reached the phone first.
I took messages between the houses
and imagined her on late Saturday afternoons,
listening, like her neighbours, for wings
circling above the line of rooftops.

### ii

He'd sit in the car, around the corner,
its nose poking out of the gravelled private drive
onto the main road, towards the girls school –
just enough to see the steps to her flat,
his camera on the passenger seat,
fitted with flash, a window down to stop the others
misting up. He'd be there at least three times a week,
from around seven when she arrived back from work.
More towards Christmas, she said.
One night she persuaded me to tell him to go home.
He was all dressed up as if he was off to the pub,
twisting that gold and garnet ring she'd given him
around his little finger, with blood on the collar
of his check shirt from where he'd just shaved.

## BLACK SLINGBACKS

On the 18th floor, looking over miles of estates,
I thought I could see hills with trees on.
As if the edge of a city was that easy to define.
At night, it's like every picture you've ever seen
of skyscrapers. If I'd been there longer,
perhaps I'd be able to name
those three blocks together, the long cliffs
by Elephant and Castle. But I never smelled
chocolate from the biscuit factory,
vinegar from Sarsons, which Carolyn said
rose sweet and sour on the wind
with the sound of trains.
One night I tried my key in the door
but it was locked from inside
and when you opened, like a gaoler,
I saw the shoes. "I've got a friend here, I'm sorry."
You didn't think I'd be back.
The date's in my cheque book.
£7, taxi, the 24th.

## BLISTERS

She feels the sun fall through the window
on the top of her head as if she's up against
an oven door. The girl on the bed's
silent as concrete or a boot,
as if she'd already been shuffled
into the threatened bin bags;
heavy chunks of muscle and fat,
jaw, thigh, shoulderblade bones scored

with the lines of a well used axe.
Toothless now as her grandmother
her dry, empty mouth is ringed
with blisters. But even when she's lit
up like a witch she'll live for days
her skin barely keeping her bones in,
eyes answering yes and no
to her gentle interrogators.

## FLOODS
*for Giya*

Our stream went under the road
in a drainage pipe, too small
for a proper bridge. But overnight
it was a river, in the garden,
sweeping away bulbs and plastic chairs.

Paras invaded the cul de sac, bringing
lorry loads of sandbags from Aldershot.
Our mothers made them tea and flirted
away worries about parquet lifting
up, ruined three piece suites.

It wasn't like the flat, clean,
silvery water covering meadows,
with swans on; smooth and confident,
catching the light, even at night. It wasn't
like the sea when it ignores tide levels
and empties shingle onto roads.
Our river, stolid and opaque,
wasn't even that fast, it just expanded,
needing more room.

When it went down, the willows
had buffers of mud, twigs and grass,
as if the birds had taken to building
estates too. The lawn was sticky
with silt as a pub floor.

A residents' committee was formed
to talk to the water company.
The drainage pipe became our camp
because we had seen what it could do.

# METEORITE STORM

After the eleventh shooting star
I say, “We’ll never be that lucky.”
But you’ve made your wishes.
I look instead at the sea,
boats moving out of port
towards a horizon which will slowly merge
with the sky. One night, such stars
strapped to masts may be the only lights
we have to count each other by.

# DAWN

*for Risenga*

The bath's hot as I can bear, I'm instructed
not to lock the door. I've been pacing corridors
and counting stairs between floors 10 and 13,
as if I'm back at school, reciting times table.

The wards are warm, beds cosy as four-posters,
cocooned in curtains. Phoning you, I gasp, "Please
come now," breathing deep as if I've forgotten
something. At a window overlooking the sea

I watch silver lights shoot along the pier,
orange headlights cruising east. The stomach-churning
ride which left me dizzy for two hours fires
red and green tracers into the waves.

I move distractedly between bed and view
like someone weighing up an extravagance.
A noise from my gut decides for me. I suck
the gas pipe as if my lungs might collapse.

You wipe my face while the midwife cleans away shit.
I'll do anything I'm told. His head moves forward and back
the way bodies surge in a tug of war. You count
seven cries. The sun is just starting to wash the sky.

## TAXIDERMY

The label says it's a mermaid.
There's always someone outside the shop
looking. It's a local sight
this Victorian glass case next to a lawnmower
and worn cutlery. Small, shrivelled,
the head is hardly a woman's, more like a dog,
although the body's that of a fish.

It was a sailor's once. Perhaps he bought it
wanting to believe there were women
of a kind at sea, craving something new
to take home. When he died,
his things were sold in a lot to the pawnshop –
the only one left in North End
and still doing good business.

Close up, it's shabby, like a large cat in a museum
with worn skin and whose eyes, though plastic or glass,
seem confused by stillness.
Just as a sailor would miss the sea
when he grew too old
and all that was left was to walk by the funfair,
watch the hovercraft take off, its skirt flapping,
or go to a pub on the dock
where the landlord kept whippets
with eyes brown as his mermaid's.

# FOOTPRINT

It may be barefoot, a clue to standing upright
or body size
it may be the first footprint in the world
walking a plain
it may be outside a window, a muddle of curves
and ridges
it may be taped off in orange, to be cast
in plaster of paris
it may be a child's washed away in waves,
lighter than water
it may be forgotten, roots cracking the soles,
disturbing the toes
it may be so quick, sink so deep in dust,
a boot will leave no trace.

## SPA TOWN

We planned to pass through
but stay for its empty pools.
Each day the town takes its cure
and waits, as if for Communion.

Above the spring, black bees
make honey for old women
with golden teeth to sell in jars
tall as altar candles.

The country's a sketch behind glass.
But circling the castle
stirring air, the way
men cruise in cars

are four blunt winged birds.
Not eagles, they fly alone
you say. There are maggots
in our honey, eggs on the rim.

And as if to warn us,
cutting through the heat
of this afternoon, is a knife
sharpener's whistle.

# MERCURY

The trees cut out so much sun,
she tries mirrors, to trick
light into the rooms, bounce it from wall
to wall. She positions them to catch
sunrise, sunset and most hours inbetween.
During storms, in case they reflect
lightning too, she turns them to the
wall. Now wherever she goes
she sees herself and the back of her head.
They cover the house, brass framed
and wood, long, square, round and are cleaned
once a week, with newspaper.
As she breathes on the glass
her face melts into the silver.
Then she thinks of mercury breaking up,
disappearing into cracks, taking parts of her
with it – an eye under the table,
her mouth between the floorboards.

JACKIE WILLS' *Powder Tower* is her first full length collection.

Already well known, her work has appeared in many magazines and journals including *Wide Skirt*, *The North*, *Echo Room*, *Verse*, *Honest Ulsterman* and *The Sunday Times*. Her poems have been published in *Agenda Anthology of New Poetry* (1992), *Spokes Anthology* (1993), *Virago New Poets Anthology* (1993) with a small selection *Black Slingbacks* (Slow Dancer Press) in 1992.

She has been a bass player with an avante-garde funk band. Currently earning her living as a journalist, she lives in Brighton with her musician/dancer partner and two children.